CHAMPS ONLY INC.
NOT FIRST ... YOU'RE LAST!

Publisher:
Mike Morrisroe

Editor in Chief/Writer:
Tom Zenner

Chief Designer:
Toby Thompson

Images Courtesy:
AP Images

Research Director:
Dash Zenner

Copy Editor:
Karen Brost

To purchase additional copies go to www.ChampsOnly.com

All rights reserved. Except for use in a review, the reproduction or utilization of this work in any form or by any electronic, mechanical, or other means, now known or hereafter invented, including: xerography, photocopying and recording, and in any information storage and retrieval system, is forbidden without written permission.

This book is available in quantity at special discounts for your group or organization.

For further information, contact the publisher.

Printed in the United States

Champs Only INC.
www.champsonly.com

CONTENTS

8 WINNING THE LOTTERY

16 A STAR FROM DAY ONE

24 DUNCAN & THE SPURS TITLE 1

32 BIG TIME BIG MEN

40 DUNCAN & THE SPURS TITLE 2

48 MVP! MVP!

60 DUNCAN & THE SPURS TITLES 3 & 4

72 DYNAMIC DUO

82 THE BEST BIG THREE

94 DUNCAN & THE SPURS TITLE 5

108 A STAR AMONG STARS

118 THE BEST POWER FORWARD EVER

136 PARADES AND RINGS

144 FAREWELL TO A LEGEND

FOREWORD

Tim Duncan was called boring, yet he had one of the most exciting, dynamic and impressive careers any athlete has enjoyed in any sport. Some people thought he was dull, yet those five, diamond-laden NBA Championship rings he owns can cast quite a shine on anyone taking a peek. What fans around the country learned about half-way through Tim Duncan's career is what the great fans of San Antonio knew all along: substance beats style every day of the week, and there was never a more substantive basketball player than Tim Duncan. He was the sure-fire, can't-miss phenom who was actually better than advertised. Both on and off the court. He is the quintessential team-first leader who was given gifts from above that he found ways every day to maximize. It's funny how people around Tim Duncan got a whole lot better and smarter the more they were near him. His coach was humble and intelligent enough to never consider going anywhere and always directed the ultimate praise to his big guy. Same thing with his co-stars. Most were quite happy to stay with Tim and help build a dynasty. Duncan is simply that rare individual who elevates the play and performance of an entire organization. He set the tone, he lived up to his potential every day, and he sure didn't tolerate anyone who wouldn't follow in line. That's leadership. That's greatness. That's an icon, future Hall of Famer and living legend who will forever be known as the best power forward to play the game of basketball.

Is Tim Duncan boring and dull? Depends on if you consider five NBA championships, a thousand regular season wins, over a hundred playoff wins and millions of memories for two generations of Spurs' fans boring. My guess is that Spurs fans, who I have witnessed to be quite possibly the best in the NBA, don't find five banners hanging in the AT&T Center courtesy of the gold star standard of what an NBA superstar is, too boring at all.

Enjoy this exciting book as we honor the career of Tim Duncan.

TOM ZENNER
@tomzenner

WINNING THE LOTTERY

THE SPURS PICK DUNCAN NO. 1

WINNING THE LOTTERY
THE SPURS PICK DUNCAN NO. 1

Some things are just meant to be. That is the best way to describe what transpired on May 18, 1997, when the planets aligned in a way that allowed Spurs' fans to hit the jackpot, and literally win the lottery. The Spurs had done their part on the court to try to get in position to have a shot at the transformational player every bad team in the NBA knew could immediately change their fortunes, the big kid with the great fundamentals from Wake Forest. Duncan was as polished of an NBA prospect as the league may have ever seen — mature, talented, poised and ready for greatness. The only mystery was, where would he end up? It all came down to the NBA Draft lottery, and with the third-worst record in the NBA the previous season, the Spurs had a 21.4 percent chance at getting the top spot. But it was pure luck they would need most of all, or should we say fate, to be on their side when the draft order was revealed. The Celtics had the best odds with 36 percent to nab the top pick, and the Philadelphia 76ers were the other team that was in contention. Every team in the draft lottery knew there was a franchise-changing player available, and that literally, careers would be made depending on where the ping pong balls landed. Greg Popovich would be entering his first full season as head coach of the Spurs after replacing Bob Hill 18 games into the previous season, and little did he know as he watched the proceedings in the TV studio in New Jersey that his life was about to change. Pop was there with owner Peter Holt. They watched other teams' names being called and realized when they were the last team called, all of their lives were about to change.

Tim Duncan was a San Antonio Spur. Let the magical, two-decade joy ride of excellence and success begin!

DUNCAN 21 — TIM TALK

" Oh, my God. "

- Gregg Popovich
(What he told The Boston Globe he said when he saw the Spurs would have the top pick)

DUNCAN DATA

- Gregg Popovich dropped his sandwich and the beer he was drinking when he realized the Spurs got the No. 1 pick.

- Before the draft, Duncan was fairly certain that he would be playing for Boston, based on the odds of winning the lottery.

DUNCAN 21

TIM TALK

" I was pretty sure I was coming to Boston. They had the two picks. Then the sixth pick went by and the third pick went by, both to Boston, and, all of a sudden, I kinda had a renewed interest in what was going on. Then Philly came up — and then I knew I was going to San Antonio and that was a great feeling."

- *Tim Duncan*
(What he told The Boston Globe about being selected by San Antonio)

DUNCAN DATA

- The NBA Draft lottery was not even the biggest story of that day in 1997, as the Knicks and Heat were playing Game 7 of the Eastern Conference finals.

- The Celtics had won just 15 games the previous season, in an apparent effort to tank the season in hopes of landing Duncan.

DUNCAN 21
TIM TALK

"You look at each other and you shake your head and say, 'Why did we deserve this?' So we were scared to death. For the first couple of days, it was like you didn't believe that it happened. Where do we start with this guy? My God, this is such a good player, we can't screw this up."

- Gregg Popovich
(What he told The Boston Globe about how he and his wife Erin reacted that night at dinner, after the 1997 draft lottery)

DUNCAN MAKES IMMEDIATE IMPACT

A STAR FROM DAY ONE
DUNCAN MAKES IMMEDIATE IMPACT

On paper, Tim Duncan looked like the safest selection you could make in the history of the NBA Draft. On the court, he was even better than any fan or team coach or official could have dreamed he would be. It was easy to see why the Celtics banked a whole season on a tank job to try to get him. But it was the Spurs who called his name first on June 25th, 1997 and Duncan wasted little time showing the world he was worth the No. 1 overall pick. When he paired with David Robinson to form one of the most epic front lines in NBA history, the Spurs were transformed from a 20-win failure to a 56-win powerhouse. It was one of the most dramatic and incredible turnarounds in NBA history, and Duncan led the way. His rookie season was incredible, as he averaged over 21 points, 12 rebounds and over two blocks per game, and here's what was may be most impressive: Duncan shot 55 percent from the field in his rookie season. Has there ever been a more savvy and skilled rookie ever? Duncan's combination of intelligence, court sense and maturity was on display in every game, and it somehow blinded viewers to just how incredibly talented he was because he just made the game look easy. Always in control, never over-matched, Duncan took the league by storm his first season and was a near-unanimous selection for the 1998 Rookie of the Year Award, earning 113 of 116 first place votes. Duncan was also named to the First Team All-NBA Team, the first rookie to do that since Larry Bird in 1980. Spurs' fans were delirious with excitement. The can't-miss kid was even better than advertised. If he was this good, this early, what was the ceiling on the career of Tim Duncan? Fans of the Spurs would be witnesses to the answer to that question, and as dominant as this once-in-a-generation rookie was in his debut season, the best part was still coming. His rookie season was a great preview. An incredible debut for the man who would eventually become the greatest to ever play his position. But as we all learned over the next 18 years, we hadn't seen anything yet.

DUNCAN DIGITS:
1997-98 SEASON:
- 21.1 Points
- 11.9 Rebounds
- 2.7 Assists
- 2.5 Blocks

DUNCAN 21 · TIM TALK

"I just hope to make a difference."

- *Tim Duncan*
(Talking before his first season with the Spurs)

DUNCAN DATA

- Tim Duncan was named the 1998 NBA Rookie of the Year.
- Duncan picked up 113 of 116 first place votes for Rookie of the Year.
- Keith Van Horn picked up the other three Rookie of the Year first place votes.
- Duncan incredibly was named Rookie of the Month for every month of his first season.

DUNCAN 21 — TIM TALK

"I've seen the future and he wears No. 21."

- **Charles Barkley**
(Talking about Duncan after seeing him play a preseason game in his rookie season)

DUNCAN DATA

- Tim Duncan's rookie season was so impressive, he finished fifth in MVP voting behind future Hall of Famers Michael Jordan, Karl Malone, Gary Payton and Shaquille O'Neal.

- The Spurs won just 20 games in the season before Duncan arrived, and finished with 56 wins in his rookie year.

- The Spurs lost to Utah in the Western Conference semifinals.

DUNCAN 21

TIM TALK

" Do I give a speech or something? "

- *Tim Duncan*
(Talking in his understated way during the Rookie of the Year news conference)

DUNCAN &
NBA CHAMPS

DUNCAN & THE SPURS
NBA CHAMPS - TITLE NO. 1 - 1998-99

When Tim Duncan arrived as a Spur, it meant one thing for San Antonio city officials: they needed to start finding some effective parade routes because there were going to be a lot of celebrations, and a lot of fans wanting to come out for the party during his career. He was so good, so early, that it was so clear to see that he would be the absolute perfect foundation to build a championship dynasty around. In Duncan's second season, he led the Spurs to their first championship, and put the rest of the NBA on notice that it was going to be a regular occurrence during his amazing career. The 1998-99 NBA season was an odd one in the sense that a lockout reduced the season to a 50-game schedule. That meant teams played a lot of back-to-back-to-back games, which means the younger the legs, the better prepared a team would be. So many things stood out in this season, and at the top of the list was just the unbelievable consistency that Duncan showed for such a young player. He put up essentially the same numbers as the previous season: almost 22 points, 12 boards and almost three blocks per game. The Admiral was healthy this season, and what a dynamic duo they were. Duncan led the Spurs to 37 wins, and San Antonio breezed through the playoffs, beating Minnesota, the Lakers and Portland in the western conference playoffs, then taking out the Knicks 4-1 in the NBA Finals. The Spurs had their first championship in franchise history. Tim Duncan was the second-youngest MVP of the Finals at the age of 23, and this playoff run for the Spurs made it clear that not only was this Tim Duncan's team in San Antonio, but he was serving notice in his quiet and dignified way that he was taking over the NBA, as well. It was time to find out where that parade route through San Antonio was going to lead! Fire up the floats. There was a champion in town..

DUNCAN DIGITS:

REGULAR SEASON:
21.7 Points
11.4 Rebounds
2.4 Assists

DUNCAN 21

TIM TALK

"It's a blessing to do what we did, and there's no guarantee we'll ever get back here."

- *Tim Duncan*
(What he said after clinching the championship in the NBA Finals)

DUNCAN DIGITS:

NBA FINALS:
27.4 Points
14 Rebounds
2.4 Assists

DUNCAN DATA

- Tim Duncan was named to the All-NBA First Team along with Karl Malone, Alonzo Mourning, Allen Iverson and Jason Kidd.

- Duncan was on the First Team All-Defensive team in 1999.

- The Spurs actually got off to a slow start in the season, going 6-8 in February, but Duncan led them to 31 wins in their final 36 games.

DUNCAN 21 — TIM TALK

> "The way Duncan is playing, there isn't a man on the planet who can stop him."
>
> - **Knicks coach Jeff Van Gundy**
> *(Talking about having to face Duncan in the Finals)*

DUNCAN DATA

- A lockout cancelled the first three months of the season, and every team played 50 games starting in January.
- Duncan led the Spurs to the No. 1 seed in the west for the playoffs.
- The Spurs lost only two playoff games in their four series.
- The NBA championship for the Spurs was their first in franchise history, and it was also their first-ever trip to the NBA Finals.

DUNCAN 21 — TIM TALK

"He'll improve in a lot of ways, because he's a guy like Magic Johnson, who wants to add to his game. I think Tim will do the same thing. Nobody thought Magic would be able to shoot a 3-point shot. Tim's got the same sort of competitive spirit. He wants to be the best."

- Gregg Popovich
(Talking about how Duncan is always looking to get better)

STARS ON & OFF THE COURT

BIG TIME BIG MEN
STARS ON & OFF THE COURT

They were the 1-2 punch that came out of a teammate test tube. It would be hard to conceive a better combo of big men in the NBA than what Spurs' fans were treated to with David Robinson and Tim Duncan. First class citizens, exemplary role models, phenomenal teammates, consummate leaders, dominating superstars. The NBA had never seen anything like it before and will never experience it again. Duncan and The Admiral were once-in-a-generation players that came along twice in a generation. Spurs' fans were smart enough to know how lucky they were to witness greatness in action for over almost 30 straight years, and it resulted in setting the foundation for a franchise that will live on for decades. Ironically, it was an injury to Robinson that allowed the Spurs to struggle mightily for one season, thus opening the door for San Antonio having the opportunity to draft Duncan in 1997. It was an anomaly, a team that already had one of the Top 50 players in NBA history who was still an elite performer, being able to draft another. The dynamic duo that launched a dynasty in San Antonio was together for the first time in Duncan's rookie season, and it resulted in 56 wins. The next year, the Spurs were even better, winning the NBA championship and continuing to play as teammates through the 2003 season. In 2000, Duncan suffered a torn lateral meniscus in his left knee late in the season, and with that injury there was no chance of a repeat, as the Spurs only won one game and were beaten in the first round of the playoffs. It made sense to rest Duncan and let him heal, and he returned in 2001 as strong as ever, earning All-NBA First Team once again. Duncan was clearly the star of the team and probably the best player in the NBA, but Robinson was still a contributor, as much with his encouragement, leadership and advice as with his on-court production. The final season together for Duncan and Robinson was the 2003 season, the year the Spurs won their second NBA title. Their final game together was June 15, 2003, in Game 6 of the NBA Finals against New Jersey. One Hall of Fame era was over. The other was really just getting started.

DUNCAN DIGITS:

POINTS PER GAME:
Tim Duncan: 19
David Robinson: 21.1

DUNCAN 21 — TIM TALK

"For a second there on the court, the last couple of seconds, I really thought, 'You know what, I'm not going to play with this guy again. I'm going to have to come out on this court without him. It's going to be weird."

- *Tim Duncan*
(Talking about playing his final game ever with Robinson after the 2003 NBA Finals)

DUNCAN DATA

NBA MVP Awards:
- Tim Duncan: 2
- David Robinson: 1

All-NBA First Team:
- Tim Duncan: 10
- David Robinson: 4

All-Defensive 1st Team:
- Tim Duncan: 8
- David Robinson: 4

All-Star Games:
- Tim Duncan: 15
- David Robinson: 10

DUNCAN DIGITS:

REBOUNDS PER GAME:
Tim Duncan: 10.8
David Robinson: 10.6

DUNCAN DIGITS:

TOTAL POINTS:
Tim Duncan: 26,496
David Robinson: 20,790

DUNCAN 21

TIM TALK

" That's cool. "

- *Tim Duncan*
(Talking after winning Game 6 of the 2003 NBA Finals with David Robinson when told his stat line was 21 points, 20 rebounds, 10 assists and 8 blocks)

THE SPURS
TITLE NO. 2 · 2002-2003

DUNCAN & THE SPURS
NBA CHAMPS - TITLE NO. 2 - 2002-2003

If there's one thing that never, ever goes out of style, it's winning championships. Tim Duncan led the Spurs to their first championship in 1999, and everyone in the franchise was starving for another. No question the Spurs team in 2003 was loaded with talent, and with Duncan's new sidekicks, Tony Parker and rookie Manu Ginobili, getting their co-starring roles down pat, there was nothing that could slow down this budding juggernaut. The Spurs ran roughshod over the NBA in 2003, and Duncan led the way in one of his finest seasons in San Antonio. The Spurs put up an NBA-best record of 60-22 in a season that was historic and monumental for many reasons. For one thing, there was a new arena, named the SBC Center at the time, now, of course, called the AT&T Center, and it was only fitting that in a building that Duncan essentially helped build with his sheer presence in San Antonio, he was able to hang a banner in it during the first year it was open. Watching Duncan perform in this season was like watching a maestro in the absolute peak of his career conduct a world-class orchestra while playing the cello and oboe at the same time. Every time he took the floor, there was a mismatch at the power forward position. Spurs' fans were absolutely treated to greatness on a nightly basis. There were some games in this epic season where Duncan's performance simply defied logic, none more so than the clinching game of the NBA Finals against New Jersey. The box score should be framed and on display at the Smithsonian, it was so incredibly dominating. Duncan closed out the series with 21 points, 20 rebounds, 10 assists and 8 blocked shots in Game 6. He put together one of the most memorable NBA Finals performances ever.

Duncan was brilliant throughout the title-winning season of 2003, the second championship for San Antonio. Of course, he was also as non-flashy as ever, living up to his ever-growing reputation for being dull. If Duncan was dull, Spurs' fans were hoping for continued boredom for many years to come!

DUNCAN 21 — TIM TALK

"I told him he was incredible. Nothing else needed to be said."

- *Steve Kerr*
(What Duncan's former teammate said after Game 6 of the NBA Finals)

DUNCAN DATA

- Tim Duncan became just the seventh player in NBA history to be named MVP of the NBA Finals twice.

- The Spurs beat the Nets in the 2003 NBA Finals, the first championship played by two former ABA teams.

- Duncan was named the MVP of the NBA, along with All-NBA First Team and All-Defensive First Team.

- Tim Duncan and David Robinson were named Sports Illustrated's 2003 "Sportsmen of the Year."

DUNCAN DIGITS:

2002-03 SEASON:
23.3 Points
12.9 Rebounds
3.9 Assists

DUNCAN 21

TIM TALK

" We just always expect a great, great game from him and he just delivered time and time again. He carried us through almost every time. We just had to provide the help for him. "

- David Robinson
(Talking about Duncan's performance in Game 6 of the NBA Finals in 2003)

DUNCAN DIGITS:

2003 NBA PLAYOFFS:
24.7 Points
11.4 Rebounds
5.3 Assists

DUNCAN DATA

- Duncan averaged over 24 points and 17 rebounds during the NBA Finals.

- The retirement of Robinson following this season allowed Duncan to flourish even more and it also ensured bigger roles for Parker and Ginobili.

- Following the 2003 championship season, Tim Duncan signed a new seven-year, $122 million contract to stay with the Spurs.

DUNCAN 21

TIM TALK

" He's the best player in the league. Once you start watching him a lot, you learn to appreciate his game even more. "

- *Speedy Claxton*
(Talking about Duncan's dominance)

BACK TO BACK MVP SEASONS

MVP! MVP!
BACK TO BACK MVP SEASONS

When you are universally acclaimed as the best basketball player in the world, an unselfish icon in the middle of his prime who also finds time to lead his team to multiple NBA championships, you generally collect a lot of hardware. That was no doubt the case for Tim Duncan in the early 2000's. The big fella was rolling, picking up back-to-back MVP awards following the 2002 and 2003 seasons. His first MVP trophy was handed over on May 9, 2002. Now keep in mind that heading into this season, Duncan had already been named All-NBA First Team five times in five seasons. He had four All-NBA Defensive first team trophies on display, and was the Rookie of the Year his first season. As great as he had been since the moment he set foot in the league, 2002 was a special season, as he put up career-high numbers with over 25 points and 12 rebounds per game, leading the Spurs to a 58-24 record. They would eventually lose in the playoffs to the Lakers, who went on to win the NBA championship that season.

On May 4, 2003, Duncan picked up his second and final MVP award, after a season in which he pumped in over 23 points per game and was third in the NBA with 13 rebounds per night. It was a season that few, if any, players in NBA history have matched, as Duncan also led the Spurs to the NBA championship and was named the Finals MVP. It takes an incredibly special and unique talent to maintain the level of excellence needed to dominate your sport to where you are voted the most valuable player in your league. Winning the award in consecutive seasons is one of the most impressive accomplishments in Tim Duncan's career, yet hardly surprising. It's another measuring stick used to determine and confirm that he, indeed, was the greatest power forward in NBA history. If you need any more reminders of that fact, the highlight reels from the 2001-02 and 2002-03 seasons will confirm it. Spurs fans had a front row seat to watch history being made by a true champion and the living embodiment of an MVP.

DUNCAN DIGITS:

2002 MVP SEASON:
25.5 Points
12.7 Rebounds
3.7 Assists

DUNCAN 21 — TIM TALK

" In my wildest dreams, I never thought I would get this far or accomplish this much. I started the season knowing I wanted to have the best season of my career. This was kind of a goal in mind. Just to win it and see it now, to accomplish it, means so much. "

- *Tim Duncan*
(Talking after being named the NBA's MVP in 2002)

DUNCAN DATA

- Tim Duncan is one of just 10 players to win the MVP award in the NBA in consecutive seasons.

- Michael Jordan was the last player to win back-to-back MVP awards in 1990-91 and 1991-92.

- Duncan beat out Jason Kidd in the balloting in 2002, and outvoted Kevin Garnett in 2003.

DUNCAN 21 — TIM TALK

> "We're thrilled for Tim. All the candidates were fantastic this season, so Tim really feels humbled by it."
>
> — *Gregg Popovich*
> (Talking about his star player being named MVP in 2002)

DUNCAN DATA

- The results in 2002 were controversial, as Nets' coach Byron Scott said the wrong player won the award.

- Duncan joins David Robinson as the only MVP winners in Spurs' history.

- Duncan finished second in MVP voting after the 2001 season, just narrowly missing out on winning the award three seasons in a row.

DUNCAN DIGITS:

2003 MVP SEASON:
23.3 Points
12.9 Rebounds
3.7 Assists

DUNCAN 21

TIM TALK

" This guy encompasses everything that you want in an MVP. I've never been more impressed watching a guy every day and playing with a guy more so than I have been with Tim Duncan. "

- *Sean Elliott*
(Talking about the impact of Tim Duncan in San Antonio after his MVP season in 2003)

DUNCAN 21 | TIM TALK

"We have so much in common. I feel very flattered (to be compared with you). You've played hard, played smart, won championships. And I don't think you're done with that."

- **Bill Russell**
(What the Hall of Fame legend said on an NBA video about Duncan)

DUNCAN DATA

- Duncan was named "Player of the Week" five times in 2002 and "Player of the Month" in December, March and April.

- In 2003, Duncan was the "Player of the Week" winner five times and scored 30 or more points 16 times during the season.

- When Duncan won his first MVP award, he had already been named All-NBA First Team five times, was the Finals MVP, Rookie of the Year, and had four All-Defensive First Team trophies.

DUNCAN 21 — TIM TALK

"In a sports world gone mad with narcissism, Duncan is a two-time MVP who eyes a camera as if it were a poisonous snake."

- *Jack McCallum of Sports Illustrated*
(What he wrote about Duncan after his MVP seasons)

DUNCAN DATA

- Duncan averaged a career high at the time 25.5 points, and 12.7 rebounds his first MVP season, and led the Spurs to a 58-24 record for the second straight year.

- Duncan's second MVP award gave him one more than David Robinson.

- Part of the reason Duncan was named MVP was the fact he led the Spurs to the best record in the NBA in 2003.

DUNCAN &
NBA CHAMPS

THE SPURS
TITLES NO. 3 & 4
2004-05 · 2006-07

DUNCAN & THE SPURS
NBA CHAMPS - TITLES NO. 3 & 4 - 2004-05 - 2006-07

As Tim Duncan's career progressed, so did the Spurs' dynasty. With the core nucleus of Duncan, Manu Ginobili and Tony Parker, and, of course, head coach Gregg Popovich leading the way, the Spurs were in contention to win an NBA championship every single season. If not for a miracle shot by Derek Fisher of the Lakers in 2004, they might have hung a banner in that season, and the Spurs came into the 2004-05 season ready to make a run at franchise title number three. The regular season was a tune up, as the Spurs rolled to a 59-23 record. The big three core was really coming into its own, fully used to playing with each other and showing off a chemistry and cohesiveness that is hard to achieve. The Western Conference playoffs were nothing but a speed bump for the eventual champions, as the Spurs lost just four games in the first three rounds. They moved on to the NBA Finals to face the defending NBA Champion Pistons. It would turn into a seven-game battle, a war that took every ounce of energy the Spurs could muster against the tough and defensive-minded team from Detroit. The Spurs had earned home court advantage, thank goodness, and they relied on their incredible crowd to help get them over the top in Game 7. For the first time in a Finals series, Duncan was not at 100 percent, which is probably why it took seven games to beat the Pistons. Duncan had missed 12 of the last 16 games of the regular season, and the ankle injury proved to be a nagging one in the postseason. But this was Tim Duncan we're talking about. Despite the sore ankle, he found a way to elevate his game even further, putting

DUNCAN DIGITS:

2004-05 REGULAR SEASON:
20.3 Points
11.1 Rebounds

DUNCAN 21 — TIM TALK

"It never gets old. It never gets old."

- *Tim Duncan*
(Talking after winning championships)

DUNCAN & THE SPURS
NBA CHAMPS – TITLES NO. 3 & 4 – 2004-05 – 2006-07

up monster numbers in the postseason and setting the stage for the all-or-nothing Game 7 finale. When the Spurs needed their big man, Duncan responded like he always does. With the game, season and championship on the line, he exploded in the second half for 17 of his 25 points, whipping the Spurs crowd into an absolute frenzy. The Spurs won that game 81-74 for NBA championship number three. Of course, Duncan was voted the MVP of the NBA Finals for a third time, joining Michael Jordan, Magic Johnson and Shaquille O'Neal in the rarest of rarified air.

The next season was a painful one for Duncan, as he played the season with plantar fasciitis in his right foot, but still found a way to lead the Spurs to a 63-19 record, which was a franchise best at the time. NBA championship number four for Duncan and the Spurs franchise came in the 2006-07 season. The Spurs had to survive a real fight against Steve Nash and the Phoenix Suns before advancing to the NBA Finals, where they swept away a young LeBron James and his over-matched Cleveland team. The resume of Tim Duncan was incredible before his latest two titles. Now he was entering the company of the NBA's all-time greats, and the difference between Tim Duncan and those very few other icons who will go down as being on the list of the greatest players of all time? Duncan wasn't finished.

DUNCAN DIGITS:
2004-05 PLAYOFFS:
23.6 Points
132.4 Rebounds

DUNCAN 21 — TIM TALK

"[Duncan's] complete game is so sound, so fundamental, so unnoticed at times, because if he didn't score, people think, 'Well, he didn't do anything.' But he was incredible and he was the force that got it done for us."

- *Gregg Popovich*
(Talking about Duncan's impact even when he doesn't score)

DUNCAN DATA

- Tim Duncan was the NBA Finals MVP for a third time in 2005.

- Duncan was named to the All-NBA First Team in 2005 and elected to the All-Defensive First Team again.

- The Spurs won the title in 2005 despite Tim Duncan being hobbled with an ankle injury that he suffered March 20th against Detroit.

DUNCAN 21 — TIM TALK

"(Duncan) is the ultimate winner, and that's why they're so good. I hate saying it, but he's the best player in the game."

- **Phoenix coach Mike D'Antoni**
(Talking about Duncan after being eliminated in the 2005 playoffs)

DUNCAN DIGITS:

2006-07 PLAYOFFS:
21.7 Points
11.2 Rebounds

DUNCAN DIGITS:

2006-07 REGULAR SEASON:
20.0 Points
10.6 Rebounds

DUNCAN DATA

- Duncan's Finals MVP award in 2005 made him just the third player to ever win the award three times.

- The 2007 championship was the first time that Tim Duncan was not named the Finals MVP, as he garnered just one vote.

- Tony Parker had the hot hand in the Finals for the Spurs, and Duncan allowed him to carry the team and earn MVP in 2007 against Cleveland.

DUNCAN 21 — TIM TALK

"Tim [Duncan] is a player for the ages. I'm a tennis fan, and Pete Sampras is one of the greats. OK, he wasn't Andre Agassi or John McEnroe. He just happens to be one of the greatest players of all time."

- *Former NBA Commissioner David Stern*
(Talking about how Duncan might not be flashy but is still spectacular)

DUNCAN DATA

- In the 2007 championship season, Duncan was once again on the All-NBA First Team and was All-Defensive First Team, as well.

- Since entering the NBA in 1997, Duncan has been a First Team All-NBA selection seven times.

- The third championship for the Spurs was the first without David Robinson and with Tony Parker and Manu Ginobilii.

- With their fourth championship, the Spurs joined the Bulls as the only teams to have at least 4 NBA championships without losing one.

DUNCAN 21 — TIM TALK

"A lot of athletes would have crumbled under that type of pressure, but he came out in that second half and showed unbelievable championship character. I'm so proud of him because he just really solidified himself as one of the top couple of power forwards ever. I mean, unbelievable character -- just awesome."

- David Robinson
(Talking about the performance of Tim Duncan in Game 7 of the 2005 NBA Finals)

DYNAMIC DUO

DUNCAN AND POPOVICH

DYNAMIC DUO
DUNCAN AND POPOVICH

There are certain coach and player relationships in the NBA that just work. They seem ordained, like you can't imagine the coach having a different star, or the iconic athlete having a different leader. Tim Duncan and Gregg Popovich are like that. They have literally been joined at the hip, forever linked to one another through fate, good fortune and the intelligence of knowing what a good thing they had together. Popovich is smart enough to know how fortunate he was to have his career linked with Duncan. They arrived at almost the same time, with Pop taking over as head coach for part of the year before Duncan arrived. When the Spurs won the draft lottery in New Jersey in May of 1997, Popovich was out there with the Spurs contingent, and immediately knew his life would never be the same because of the planets aligning for that one night. Spurs general manager R. C. Buford is another person whose career was partly made because of the fact that Tim Duncan was a Spur, and he sums up the Duncan and Pop dynamic as well as anyone in an interview he did with *The New York Times*:

"I think this term is often overused, but there are very few relationships where the relationship between player and coach can be described as a real soul mate. But we've been fortunate enough that Pop and Tim are connected that way. When things are tough, they've got that. That's their rock."

Don't underestimate how important it's been that both the coach and player understood this. Oftentimes

DUNCAN 21 — TIM TALK

> "Timmy's a pain in the ass, and I'm tired of coaching him. Anybody else (have questions)? Good. Have a good day."
>
> *- Gregg Popovich*
> (What he jokingly said to the media in 2013)

DYNAMIC DUO
DUNCAN AND POPOVICH

ego takes over, with either or the coach, or player, or both wanting to go somewhere and try to prove that the shared success they had in one place is something that could be duplicated on their own. It rarely works out that way. This coach and player made each other better. Made each other legends. Gregg Popovich coaches players hard, and that included his first-ballot Hall of Famer wearing the No. 21 jersey. The fact that Tim Duncan was professional enough to allow his coach to treat him like he would any other player created a culture in the Spurs locker room and on that team that nobody was above being expected to do his job right all the time. It's just another example, along with taking less money to create salary space for other players, that shows what an unselfish, team-first winner Tim Duncan is. As great as a player as Duncan is, it's hard to imagine him having the type of career he had without Pop there to guide it. Likewise, it's impossible to imagine Popovich experiencing, even remotely, the same amount of success coaching in Orlando or Milwaukee or Los Angeles or Boston or anywhere else. Never, ever, in the history of sports have a player and coach been more perfect for each other. Similar demeanor, similar competitiveness, similar desire to win, and similar senses of humor. It was a match made in heaven, and it resulted in five NBA championships, a lifetime of memories for Spurs fans, and a part of sports history that will never be replicated.

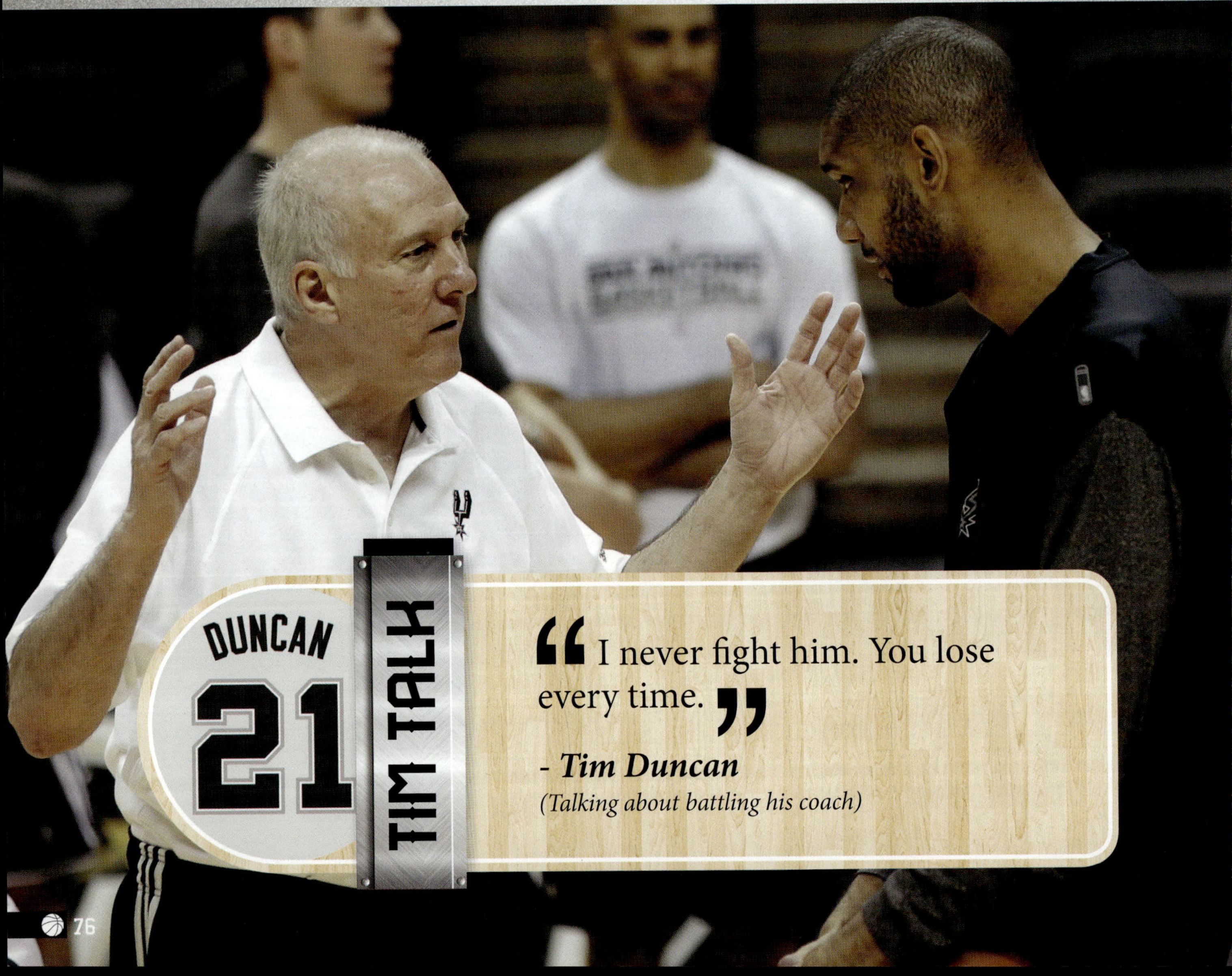

DUNCAN 21 | TIM TALK

> " I never fight him. You lose every time. "
>
> - *Tim Duncan*
> (Talking about battling his coach)

DUNCAN 21 — TIM TALK

"It's almost like a father-son relationship. Pop gets mad at Tim. Tim gets mad at Pop. But at the end of the day, they don't go to bed mad at each other."

- *Michael Finley*
(Talking to espn.com about the dynamics of the coach and player relationship)

DUNCAN 21 — TIM TALK

" When he's not at practice, I'm going to be little depressed, I think. It makes me sad. I'm going to miss it an awful lot. "

- Gregg Popovich
(Talking to The Washington Post in 2014 about what life will be like without Duncan)

DUNCAN DATA

- In Duncan's second season, the Spurs got off to a 6-8 start and many fans were clamoring for Doc Rivers to replace Pop. The Spurs eventually won their first NBA championship that season.

- In their 19 seasons together, Pop and Duncan have been a part of 1,001 wins in the regular season and playoffs.

DUNCAN DATA

- With Popovich on the bench and Duncan in the lineup, the Spurs had 17 consecutive seasons of 50 or more wins.

- The Spurs have been to the playoffs all 19 seasons that Popovich coached Duncan.

DUNCAN 21 — TIM TALK

"Tim is supercompetitive, and Pop is supercompetitive. I don't think you understand just how competitive until you're around them, but they really share that in common."

- *Del Demps*
(Talking about what Popovich and Duncan have in common)

THE BIG THREE
DUNCAN, PARKER & GINOBILI MAKE HISTORY

The one constant for the Spurs on the floor during the Tim Duncan era has been Tim Duncan himself, of course, but the cast of supporting characters and his co-stars have changed and evolved throughout his 19-year career. After David Robinson left the team in 2003, fans witnessed the rise of the Big Three, consisting of Duncan and his foreign teammates, Tony Parker from France and Manu Ginobili from Argentina. Parker and Ginobili were part of the 03 championship, but it was after that season when their games were allowed to flourish and expand, which helped the Spurs win three more titles during the rest of years they would play with Duncan. While Duncan was earning his reputation for being "boring" on the court, Parker and Ginobili were the opposite: flashy, fast, emotional, energetic. Don't underestimate for a second how difficult it would be to seamlessly incorporate two foreign players into an established culture that had one true identity and into a system where the face of the franchise was still in his prime. The indoctrination of the talented young players would not have happened if Tim Duncan did not allow it to. There were certainly trials and tribulations, and the process wasn't exactly smooth at the beginning, and even Duncan had his doubts if it would all work out. It's a credit to Duncan that he trusted the judgement of his coach, Gregg Popovich, and the Spurs front office, and allowed this transformation of the franchise to occur.

DUNCAN 21 | TIM TALK

" I think it's pretty well documented that I wasn't too sure about what to expect from (Parker). With French Boy (Ginobili), it was about him being, whatever, 13 years old and asking him to start for a team that's been doing pretty good. With Crazy Boy (Ginobili), it was just getting used to playing with someone like that. "

- Tim Duncan
(Talking to San Antonio Express News in 2010 about his early thoughts on Parker and Ginobili)

THE BIG THREE
DUNCAN, PARKER & GINOBILI MAKE HISTORY

Few, if any superstars would have allowed it with the class that Duncan displayed. He not only allowed it, he embraced it. One thing was always evident. There was never a doubt about the combined talent of these three players, and Spurs' fans were treated to the end result: three more titles, hundreds of wins and the excitement and the reality of knowing each and every season that your team was a true title contender.

The on-court chemistry the three future Hall of Famers displayed blossomed into an incredible friendship, kinship and bond. They were close on and off the court. As their roles increased and decreased over the years, they adjusted their games accordingly, morphing from a shut down defensive team into a faster, more offensive-oriented team relying on three pointers and fast breaks. Yes, Duncan may have been boring to some, Ginobili may have taken some liberties in the flopping department, and Parker could come off a little distant to outside observers, but the original Big Three played basketball with a joy and passion and effectiveness never before seen in the NBA. It's one of the things that makes sports so special: three incredibly talented people coming from different corners of the globe and ending up in a city in Texas to make magic and history together and bring a collective joy to the community that few other places have ever experienced. It was special.

DUNCAN 21
TIM TALK

> "It just happened. The most important part was just not be selfish. Try to play for a system. Don't let our egos be more important than the final goal and just try to adjust to play with each other. Then, the system was about Pop to make us all fit and have our moments. It was a combination of everybody trying to do well and create what we created."

- Manu Ginobili
(Talking to San Antonio Express News about their chemistry)

DUNCAN DATA

- In November of 2015, Duncan, Parker and Ginobili passed Larry Bird, Kevin McHale and Robert Parish of the Celtics for most wins by a threesome in NBA history.

- On the night the Spurs' Big Three set the record, they beat the Celtics in Boston, and the Big Three combined for 26 points.

- Tim Duncan, Manu Ginobili and Tony Parker have been teammates since the 2002-03 season.

DUNCAN 21 — TIM TALK

"When there is talk about the best point guards, sometimes they don't talk about me, but that's not my main motivation. They can talk about Jason Kidd, Steve Nash, Deron Williams and Chris Paul. I still have the most rings."

- *Tony Parker*
(Talking about not being mentioned in same conversations about the best point guards)

DUNCAN DATA

- The Big Three made the playoffs every single season they were together.
- Since the Big Three started playing together, they won four NBA championships.
- The Big Three won at least 50 games and had a 60 percent winning percentage in every single season they played together.

DUNCAN 21 — TIM TALK

"We would have two less championships here if it was not for Manu Ginobili. In my eyes, he's the stud of the world."

- *Gregg Popovich*
(Talking about the impact Ginobili has had on the team)

DUNCAN 21 — TIM TALK

"I always say if we did what we did in New York, we'd be gods right now."

- **Tony Parker**
(Talking about what kind of impact they would have made in NYC)

DUNCAN DATA

- While the Spurs were lucky to nab Duncan with the top pick in 1997, they deftly selected Ginobili with the 57th pick in 1999 and selected Parker 28th overall in 2001.

- The Spurs' Big Three were the first set of three or more teammates to win four titles together since Magic Johnson, Kareem Abdul-Jabbar and Michael Cooper of the Lakers.

- The Big Three combined to win 126 playoff games.

DUNCAN & NBA CHAMPS

THE SPURS
TITLE NO. 5 · 2013-14

DUNCAN & THE SPURS
NBA CHAMPS - TITLE NO. 5 - 2013-14

Tim Duncan finally did something in the 2012-13 season he never had done before. His team lost in the NBA Finals. It was a crushing, devastating blow, losing to Miami in seven games and denying Duncan and company their fifth NBA title. It would take most teams months, maybe even years to recover, but Duncan and the Spurs used it as fuel and the motivating force to try to make up for it the following season. In Duncan's 17th season in the NBA, he was surrounded by a roster that was deep and talented and adept at executing Gregg Popovich's system. They were truly a joy to watch, offensively and defensively, and while it was clear that Duncan was not the dominating force he was on every other championship team, he was still a big time contributor and the heart and soul of the roster. The Spurs won 62 games in the regular season and faced their toughest fight in the playoffs in the very first round, as they needed seven games to beat the Mavericks. After that, they ran roughshod over the rest of their competition, crushing the Blazers in five games, the Thunder in six, and dominating the Heat in their NBA Finals rematch. The Spurs average of victory in their four wins was 18 points. Payback was oh, so sweet. In what was truly ironic and a joy to behold, this edition of the San Antonio Spurs showed the world how beautiful the game of basketball can look when played properly. No longer was this a team ridiculed for boring play. It was all about teamwork, and passing, and spacing and execution. A YouTube video paid tribute to the Spurs and their artistic style of play. It was called "The Beautiful Game," and it has had millions of views. Duncan had his fifth NBA title, putting him on the same elite championship level as Magic Johnson and Kobe Bryant, passing Shaquille O'Neal on the all-time list. Duncan averaged over 15 points in the Finals, and when he would eventually be enshrined into the Basketball Hall of Fame, he would enter as not only one of the greatest players of all time, but one of the greatest winners the sport has ever seen.

DUNCAN 21 — TIM TALK

"You showed the world how beautiful this game is."

- NBA Commissioner Adam Silver
(Talking about the style of basketball the Spurs put on display)

DUNCAN DIGITS:

2013-14 SEASON:
15.1 Points
9.7 Rebounds

TIM TALK

"One more year! One more year!"

- *Spurs Fans*
(What they were shouting at Tim Duncan during the championship parade)

DUNCAN 21

DUNCAN DATA

- During this season, Duncan became the oldest player to have a 20/20 game in NBA history, as he scored 23 points and 21 rebounds on December 2nd against Atlanta.

- In that same game, Duncan scored the game-winning points on a last-second shot.

- Duncan was 38 years old and still led all players with 50 rebounds in the Finals against Miami.

DUNCAN 21 | TIM TALK

" I've thought about that play every day, without exception, four, five, six, 10 times a day. I always will. "

- *Gregg Popovich*
(Talking about using the Ray Allen 3-pointer in Game 6 of the previous Finals as motivation)

DUNCAN DATA

- During the NBA Finals, Duncan shot an astounding 57 percent from the field and averaged 15 points.

- Duncan joined John Salley as the only players in NBA history to win an NBA title in three different decades.

- The Spurs used the loss of Game 7 in the Finals the year before as motivation the entire season.

DUNCAN DATA

- There were 10 foreign players on the roster for the Spurs during this championship season.
- The Spurs were no longer a defensive-minded team, as they led the NBA in 3-point percentage and assists.
- The Spurs started the season on fire, winning 13 of their first 14 games and putting up a 19-game winning streak in March.
- Kawhi Leonard was named the MVP of the NBA Finals.

DUNCAN 21 — TIM TALK

" No. 1 team in all of sports "

- ESPN Ultimate Team Rankings
(Where ESPN ranked the Spurs in 2014 following their championship over the Heat)

DUNCAN DATA

- This edition of the Spurs was called "The Beautiful Game" Spurs, and during the Finals against Miami they passed the ball 472 more times than Miami.

- Gregg Popovich controlled the minutes of each player throughout the year, as no player played more than 30 on any night of the season.

- The Spurs set an NBA Finals record by shooting 52.8 from the field and 46.6 percent on 3s.

DUNCAN 21 — TIM TALK

" It makes last year OK. "

- *Tim Duncan*
(Talking about getting revenge on the Heat)

DUNCAN DATA

- Duncan scored 14 points, with eight rebounds, two assists and two blocked shots in the clinching Game 5 win.
- The Spurs set an NBA record with 12 wins of 15 or more points in the playoffs.
- The Spurs outscored their opponents by 214 points in the postseason.

●●●●●● **DUNCAN DIGITS:**

2013-14 PLAYOFFS:
16.3 Points
9.2 Rebounds
2.0 Assists

A STAR AMONG STARS

DUNCAN'S 15 ALL-STAR APPEARANCES

A STAR AMONG STARS
DUNCAN'S 15 ALL-STAR APPEARANCES

If there was an NBA All-Star game played during Tim Duncan's tenure with the Spurs, there's a good chance he was representing the West in it. Duncan played in 15 All-Star Games, scoring two points in his debut game in 1998 and also scoring a bucket in his final game in 2015. In an ironic twist of fate, Duncan's first and last All Star Games were both played in New York City. He made his presence felt every time he suited up with his fellow stars, and always did his part in putting on a show for NBA fans around the world. Duncan was named the MVP of the All-Star Game in 2000, and had memorable moments in every single appearance.

Duncan's first All-Star Game was in Madison Square Garden, and the West was coached by George Karl. It was famous for being the only All-Star Game that featured both Kobe Bryant and Michael Jordan. Duncan was on the West team with David Robinson, and scored two points in 14 minutes of action. In 2000, the game was in Oakland, and with Duncan in the starting lineup, the West beat the East 137-126. Duncan and Shaquille O'Neal were co-MVPs of the game, and Duncan dominated the stat sheet, with 24 points and 14 rebounds. In 2001, the venue was the MCI Center in Washington, D.C., and it was the 50th All-Star-Game, which made it extra special. By this time in his career, it was a yearly tradition for Duncan to start in the game, and he led the West with 14 rebounds as the West lost 111-110. Philadelphia was the site of the 2002 All-Star Game, where the West beat the East 135-120, as Duncan

DUNCAN 21

TIM TALK

" Madison Square Garden is a really special place for me, personally. My first All-Star Game, first championship, and now another great experience here. "

- *Tim Duncan*
(Talking after his final All-Star Game in 2015)

A STAR AMONG STARS
DUNCAN'S 15 ALL-STAR APPEARANCES

once again started for the West, and showed his remarkable consistency by grabbing 14 rebounds in his third-straight game. In 2003, the West won again, this time in double overtime by a score of 155-145. The West's starting lineup was exactly the same as the previous year, and Duncan once again drew over a million votes from fans across the world and grabbed 15 rebounds for the victorious West. The All-Star Game moved to the West Coast in 2004, as the Staples Center hosted the showcase, again won by the Western All-Stars, 136-122. Duncan led the West in rebounding yet again, with a game-high 13. In 2005 in Denver, Duncan was in the starting lineup again for the West, and was joined in the game by his head coach Gregg Popovich as the West dropped the game to the East 125-115. Duncan had 15 points and nine rebounds and nearly had as many fan votes as Kobe Bryant. Duncan got to play his first All-Star Game in the state of Texas the following year, as Houston was the host city for the 55th-annual game. The West dropped a close one, 122-120, as Duncan had 15 points and 10 rebounds in his eighth All-Star showcase. In 2007, it was another start, another win, and another solid performance for Duncan in Las Vegas. The West crushed the East 153-132. New Orleans was the site of the game in 2008, a memorable weekend that culminated with a 134-128 win by the East. Duncan had four points and nine rebounds in the win for the West. By now, the days of Duncan putting up big

DUNCAN 21 — TIM TALK

" You already have one of those rings so I'm taking the trophy. "

- Shaquille O'Neal
(What he said to Duncan during the trophy presentation)

A STAR AMONG STARS
DUNCAN'S 15 ALL-STAR APPEARANCES

numbers in the All-Star Game were pretty much over, but he was still a starter in his 10th classic. Phoenix was the site of the game in 2009, a spot where Duncan had carved out a lot of great memories in classic playoff showdowns with the Suns. The West clobbered the East in this game, 146-119, as Duncan scored six points in 18 minutes of action. A crowd of over 108,000 was on hand in Arlington, Texas in 2010, as the Mavericks hosted this game at Cowboys Stadium. It was an incredible atmosphere, as the East beat the West in a thriller, 141-139. In the 2011 All-Star Game, Popovich named Duncan the All-Star starter at center for the Western Conference, replacing Yao Ming who was injured and out for the season. That allowed Duncan to start in his 12th-straight All-Star Game, which was played at Staples Center in LA, and won by the West 148-143. Duncan's next All-Star appearance came two years later, as he scored two points for the West off the bench in Houston, a game the West won 143-138. Duncan's final All-Star appearance came in New York City, which had extra meaning for Tim because he clinched his first NBA championship in that city, and played in his first NBA All-Star Game there in 1998. The coach for the West in this game was Steve Kerr, who was Duncan's teammate with the Spurs 12 years earlier.

It was a treat for Spurs' fans to be able to watch Duncan perform on the game's biggest stage each season, and it meant that in 36 of the 39 years the Spurs have been in the NBA, they have had at least one representative in the All-Star Game.

DUNCAN DATA

- Tim Duncan was named MVP of the 2000 All-Star Game. He has been named NBA Rookie of the Year, NBA MVP, NBA Finals MVP, All-Star Game MVP and Wooden Award Winner. The only other players to do that are Michael Jordan and Larry Bird.

- Duncan is one of just five players to play in 15 or more All-Star Games, joining Kareem Abdul-Jabbar, Kobe Bryant, Shaquille O'Neal and Kevin Garnett.

DUNCAN DATA

- Duncan played an All-Star Game in every NBA city in Texas except San Antonio.

- Duncan holds the all-time record for defensive rebounds in an All-Star Game history with 98.

DUNCAN DIGITS:

15 NBA ALL-STAR GAMES:
9.3 Points
9.1 Rebounds

THE BEST POWER FORWARD EVER

THE FACTS SPEAK FOR THEMSELVES

THE BEST POWER FORWARD OF ALL TIME

Tim Duncan is the best power forward to ever play in the NBA. His statistics, accomplishments and contributions to the sport confirm that. He was the can't-miss kid out of college that teams tanked a season trying to get a crack at, because deep down they knew he was a franchise changer. He personified greatness on the court and off of it, and to think he played an entire career for one team, all 19 seasons, shows that his loyalty and humble nature were equal to his talent. The beauty about Tim Duncan is that he has spent the majority of his life and all of his professional life showing people how great he is, not telling them. He never sought out the spotlight, he avoided personal attention, and he only and always wanted what was best for the team, because he knew that's what was best for him, too. They don't put players in the Hall of Fame or call you an all-time great because of the number of your Twitter followers, the amount of dunk contests you win or your ability to mesmerize in a press conference. Some people called Tim Duncan dull. Well, those are the same people that either aren't used to winning or don't enjoy it as much as Duncan does. He set out to be one of the greatest to ever play the game. Mission accomplished. For 19 years, he was the driving force and the engine behind the success of the San Antonio Spurs. Playoff appearances every season. Parades after five of them. Other players would come and go throughout his glorious 19-year career, but the Big Fundamental, as Shaquille O'Neal so adeptly named him, was the rock. As reliable as any player in the history of sports, he excelled at his craft with equal parts dominance, consistency, humility, skill and precision. There will never, ever be another Tim Duncan on the basketball court. If anyone thinks it might be possible to approach the success he's had in his career, read the next 12 pages of accomplishments, awards and records Tim Duncan has accumulated and see how you feel after that.

DUNCAN DIGITS:
REGULAR SEASON CAREER:
19.0 Points 3.0 Assists
10.8 Rebounds 2.2 Blocks

DUNCAN 21 — TIM TALK

> **"** More cutthroat than people give him credit for. I loved everything about him on the court. **"**
>
> - *Kobe Bryant*
> (Talking about how competitive Duncan was)

DUNCAN DATA

- In 19 NBA Seasons, Duncan made the playoffs every season and won five NBA Championships.

- Duncan was the MVP in 2002 and 2003, and three times was named NBA Finals MVP.

- In Duncan's final game of his career in the 2016 playoffs against OKC, he scored 19 points and pulled down five rebounds.

- Duncan and Popovich combined to win 1,001 games, the most by a player and coach in NBA history.

DUNCAN DIGITS:

PLAYOFF CAREER:
20.6 Points 3.0 Assists
11.4 Rebounds 2.3 Blocks

DUNCAN DATA

- Duncan has played with 140 different teammates in his career.

- Duncan won the Naismith Award as the best college basketball player his final year in Wake Forest, was the NBA's Rookie of the Year the following season, and NBA champion the season after that.

- The Spurs had a winning percentage of at least .600 in all 19 seasons.

- Duncan scored 26,496 points, the 14th most in NBA history.

- Duncan finished sixth all-time in rebounds in NBA history with 15,091.

DUNCAN DATA

- Duncan blocked 3,020 shots in his career, the fifth most in NBA history.

- Duncan was only ejected from one game in his career. It was in 2007 when referee Joey Crawford ejected him for laughing at him from the bench.

- In 52 career games against Kobe Bryant, Duncan and the Spurs won 31 of them.

- Duncan played 47,368 minutes, the 10th-most in NBA history.

- Duncan is one of just two players to win NBA titles in three different decades.

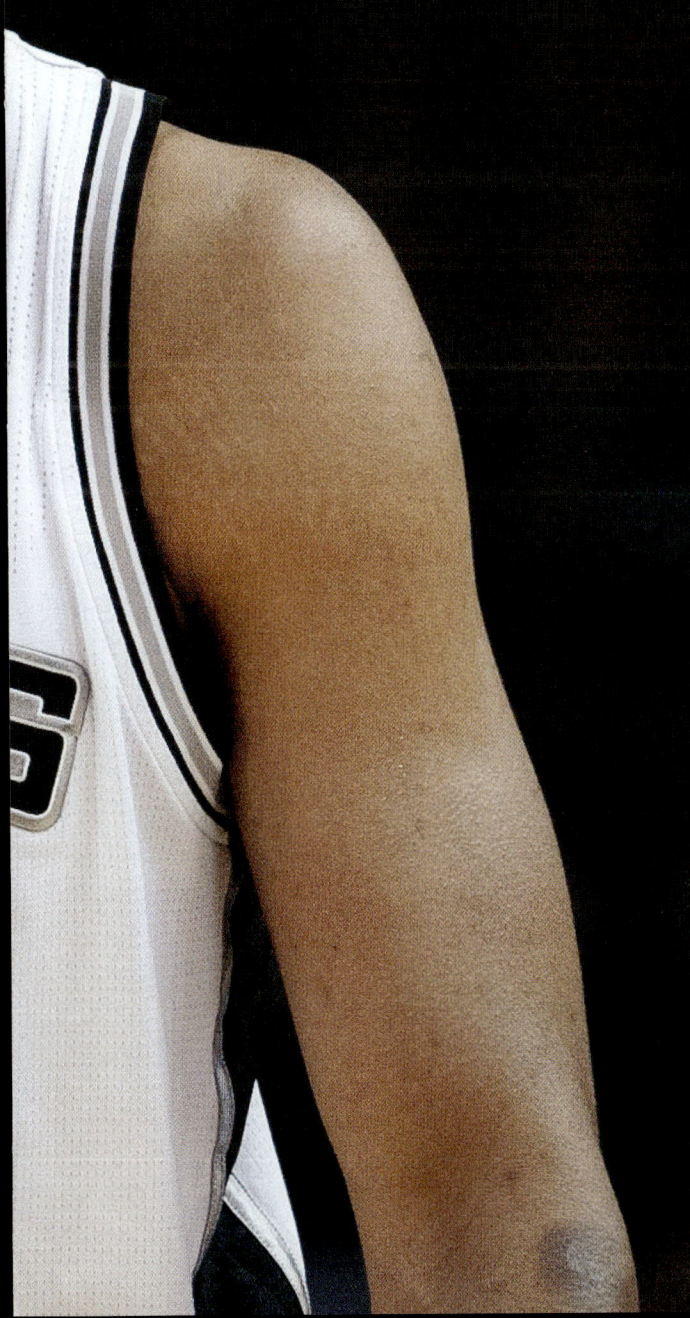

DUNCAN DATA

- The only other players to have as many seasons with the same franchise are John Stockton (19) with the Jazz and Kobe Bryant (20) with the Lakers.

- The final game Duncan would play for the Spurs was a 113-99 loss to the Thunder in the 2016 playoffs.

- According to *espn.com*, over 15 percent of Duncan's career shots were bank shots.

- According to *espn.com*, Duncan made 60 percent of the bank shots he took in his career.

DUNCAN 21 — TIM TALK

"Tim Duncan is one of the most dominant players in NBA history. His devotion to excellence and mastery of the game led to five NBA championships, two regular-season MVP awards and a place among the all-time greats, while his understated selflessness made him the ultimate teammate."

- NBA Commissioner Adam Silver
(Talking about Duncan and his impact on the game)

DUNCAN 21 — TIM TALK

"If you show excitement, then you also may show disappointment or frustration. If your opponent picks up on this frustration, you are at a disadvantage."

- **Tim Duncan**
(Talking about his stoic nature)

DUNCAN DATA

- Duncan was named to 15 All-Defensive teams, the last honor coming when he was 38 years old.

- Duncan earned over $236 million during his playing career with the Spurs, according to *spotrac.com*.

- Duncan played in 15 NBA All-Star games in his career.

- Duncan was an eight-time NBA All-Defensive First Team member.

DUNCAN DATA

- Duncan is the all-time leading scorer in Spurs' team history.
- Duncan was the Sports Illustrated's "Sportsman of the Year" in 2003.
- At Wake Forest, Duncan was named the "National College Player of the Year" in 1997.
- Duncan represented the United States in the 2004 Summer Olympics in Athens and led the team in scoring.

DUNCAN 21 | TIM TALK

"We walk into our houses and thank Tim Duncan. You think about all the coaches and all the GMs and even the assistant video guys who are now assistant coaches, all the people who have climbed the NBA ladder — we all owe our success, our place in the league to Timmy."

- *Hawks' coach Mike Budenholzer*
(What the former Spurs assistant said about Duncan's importance)

DUNCAN DATA

- Only one time in Duncan's career did the Spurs ever win fewer than 50 games. That was in the lockout-shortened 1999 season, when teams only played 50 total games. The Spurs won the NBA championship that season.

- Duncan recorded eight triple-doubles in his career, including four in the playoffs.

- Duncan was named the "Player of the Week" in the NBA 23 times.

DUNCAN DATA

- Duncan's career high for points was 53, against Dallas in 2001.
- The highest single game total for rebounds for Duncan occurred in 2010, when he grabbed 27 boards against Atlanta.
- Duncan played 251 playoff games. Eighteen NBA franchises have fewer playoff games in their history.

DUNCAN DATA

- Duncan had 835 career dunks.

- Duncan joined a list that includes Larry Bird and Kareem Abdul-Jabbar as Rookie of the Year winners who claimed an NBA title in their second season. It took Michael Jordan seven and LeBron James nine.

- According to Sportsnet, the combined attendance for Spurs regular season games Duncan played in was over 14,400,000.

DUNCAN 21 — TIM TALK

> "Trying to be something that you're not gets you out of your comfort zone. I'm not that guy. I did a little bit of that. I've done my share of it, but I'm just not that guy. I don't think of myself in that respect. I love playing basketball and that's what I want to do. I don't need the extra stuff."
>
> **— Tim Duncan**
> *(Talking about what his philosophy was)*

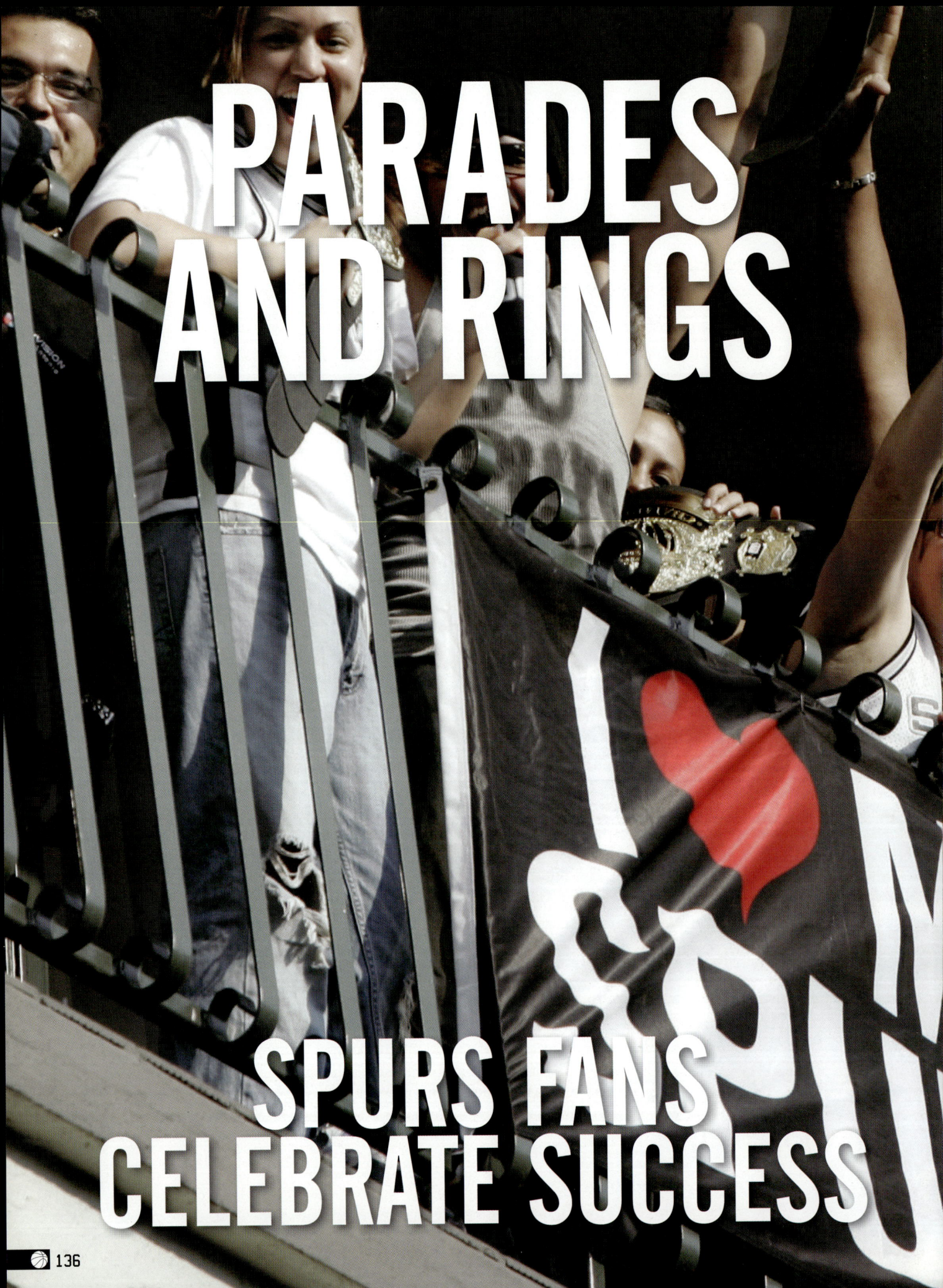
PARADES AND RINGS
SPURS FANS CELEBRATE SUCCESS

PARADES AND RINGS
SPURS FANS CELEBRATE SUCCESS

One of the most important things city officials needed to do when Tim Duncan was drafted by the Spurs in 1997 was find an appropriate parade route to celebrate the handful of NBA titles that would be coming. To put it mildly, Duncan helped put the city of San Antonio on the map as a big time professional sports city because of the success of the Spurs. The amount of exposure the city received because of Duncan and the Spurs is almost impossible to measure, but one thing is for sure. NBA fans and players know very well how tough it is to play in the Spurs arena, especially in the playoffs. The atmosphere, energy and noise level during a Spurs playoff game is off the charts. Think about many major cities, and the championship droughts they go through. Winning major championships is a very difficult thing to do, and it's not that Duncan and company made it look easy, because it never is. What they did is make it possible for it to happen every single one of his 19 seasons with the Spurs. The parades in San Antonio were such parties. So much fun for the entire city. The banner raising ceremonies, ring ceremonies, trophy presentations, visits to see the President in Washington, D.C, all of the festive things that made being a fan of the Spurs one of the coolest things in sports for the last two decades.

TIM TALK

" We've never held one of these before, this is for NBA World Champions. Lots of folks have been waiting 26 years for this moment. "

- *San Antonio City Public Information Manager Carmen Vazquez-Gonzalez*
(Talking about preparations for the parade in 1999)

DUNCAN DATA

JUNE 27, 1999

- Spurs' players rode 20 barges in the 2.5 mile parade along the River Walk.
- An estimated crowd of over 250,000 attended the celebration.
- The first championship parade lasted one hour.

DUNCAN DATA

JUNE 18, 2003
- After a barge parade down the River Walk, over 50,000 fans attended a rally at the Alamodome.

TIM TALK

"It was a lot of fun to be out there and hear all the people screaming. It was everything it was in '99. San Antonio fans are so loyal to their teams."

- *Tim Duncan*
(Talking at the celebration in 2003)

DUNCAN DATA

JUNE 25, 2005
- Over 300,000 people lined the banks of the San Antonio River, cheering on the players as they cruised on river barges.

DUNCAN 21

TIM TALK

" You guys continue to come out and support us. Hopefully, we can get another one. "

- *Tim Duncan*
(Talking to the crowd after title number four)

DUNCAN DATA

JUNE 18, 2014

- A crowd estimated at 100,000 people attended the River Walk parade along the San Antonio River.

- Fans braved temperatures of over 90 degrees as they lined up five hours before the festivities began.

TIM TALK — DUNCAN 21

" Go Spurs Go. "

- **Spurs Fans**
(What hundreds of thousands of fans chanted at all five celebrations)

FAREWELL TO A LEGEND

THE SPORTS WORLD SAYS GOODBYE

FAREWELL TO A LEGEND
THE SPORTS WORLD SAYS GOODBYE

It was one of those things that was surprising, but not shocking. Spurs' fans knew they would have to face the reality of Tim Duncan walking away from the NBA, and it happened on July 11, 2016. After 19 seasons, five championships, over a thousand wins and millions of memories, it was over. Duncan had given his heart and soul to the team and the city he called home, and left everything he had on the floor. He did it in the most dignified way possible, by simply issuing a release, followed by a letter to fans shortly after. There was no pomp and circumstance. No press conferences. Duncan went out like he played the game for almost two decades. Stoically, with class and dignity, and a whole lot of respect from everyone around him. Immediately after the news hit, the well wishes poured in. Everyone connected to the game of basketball respected Tim Duncan, and the eloquence of the tributes was incredible. Tim Duncan had made the city of San Antonio a better place. He had made the Spurs a better and more valuable franchise. He had made the NBA a better sports league. He's an ultimate winner with an incredible career that will never be duplicated.

DUNCAN 21

TIM TALK

> "Timmy D you know how I feel about you, what you did for me and for the entire NBA. Thank you for an amazing career! #BestPFEver #Legend."
>
> - @King James
> *(Tweet from LeBron James)*

DUNCAN 21

TIM TALK

"Congrats to Tim Duncan. Probably a top 5 all-time player and undoubtedly a top 5 all-time teammate. Wow, what a career."

- @SteveKerr
(Tweet from Steve Kerr)

DUNCAN 21

TIM TALK

"Congrats TD #19yrs #GoSpursGo."
- @kobebryant
(Tweet from Kobe Bryant)

TIM TALK

"Timmy D. Say it ain't so!!! Greatest power forward ever!"

— *@swish41*
(Tweet from Dirk Nowitzki)

DUNCAN 21 — TIM TALK

> "Even tho I knew it was coming, I'm still moved by the news. What a HUGE honor to have played with him for 14 seasons! #ThankYouTD"
>
> — @manuginobili
> *(Tweet from Manu Ginobili)*

DUNCAN 21 — TIM TALK

> " The BIG FUNDAMENTAL. Best Power Forward to ever lace them up. Like he has done with many before "
>
> - @kevinlove
> *(Tweet from Kevin Love)*

DUNCAN 21 — TIM TALK

> "My biggest respect and admiration for #TimDuncan. I've had the privilege to play against him in…"
>
> — **@paugasol**
> *(Tweet from Pau Gasol)*

DUNCAN 21
TIM TALK

> "Got a chance to play against Duncan for 10 years and every time I played against him I was in amazement!! Congrats on a great career!!"
>
> - **@Klow7**
> (Tweet from Kyle Lowry)

DUNCAN 21 — TIM TALK

"Upset at Tim Duncan we didn't get to honor him at a Mavs Spurs game. Happy I've had the opportunity to witness his greatness so often"

- @mcuban
(Tweet from Mark Cuban)

DUNCAN 21 — TIM TALK

" Congrats to the best power forward to ever play the game. It was truly an honor. Winner above all else. #thankyouTD "

- @blakegriffin32
(Tweet from Blake Griffin)

DUNCAN 21 — TIM TALK

"Loved calling games of @TimSlamDuncan @WakeForest & no doubt to me GOAT big forward to play in @NBA."
— **@DickieV**
(Tweet from Dick Vitale)

DUNCAN 21 — TIM TALK

"Tim Duncan retires. No statement. No letter. Just a brief Spurs release: 1,072-438 (.710) record. Five championships. Goodbye No. 21."

- @WojVerticalNBA
(Tweet from Adrian Wojnarowski)

DUNCAN 21 — TIM TALK

" #ThankYouTD, for everything. "
- *@Spurs*
(Tweet from the Spurs)